Never A Better Time Than Now

103 Poems to enhance the present

By Terry Lander

Published by Lyvit Publishing, Cornwall

www.lyvit.com

ISBN 978-0-9555061-5-4

"I try to keep stress to a minimum, as to worry about problems consumes energy available for dealing with them."

To Soapy Toes, who informs us of her mischief through her smile.

Contents

Contents

Contents

Jungle Fever

The king of the jungle stood one day
To open the meeting he'd called
The Chimpanzees were the last to hush
And the Ostriches looked appalled

He claimed his homeland was too savage
And hoped it would come to an end
Though most of the beasts that roamed ate meat
He wanted all kinds to be friends

The herbivores cheered at this great news
As the carnivores gasped and shook
The lion convinced them plants were great
They just had to go out and look

And so it was for the next few weeks
These animals passed their food by
But first they shot them a hungry smile
Assuring them they wouldn't die

At the end of a very long month
The king had achieved his mission
All carnivores ate nothing but plants
But they died of malnutrition

Sight In The Sky

A rainbow spreads across the sky
The children delight
To see this great sight
And point up as they pass me by

But I won't be smiling just yet
I'm looking to hide
By running inside
As standing out here I'll get wet

Lunching With Ladies

I'm lunching with ladies from noon until one
Although they're all laughing it isn't much fun
I'm stuck in the corner with nothing to say
And I can't go out as it's looking quite grey

They giggle at what they did at the weekend
Like shopping and clubbing or seeing a friend
But I can't join in as I'm eating my food
The whole thing's put me in a very strange mood

There isn't too long now 'til I must get back
My in-tray looks like it would fill a large sack
But I'd rather be there and see the day fly
I can't lunch with ladies because I'm a guy

Inverted

I stand on my head all day long
Each smile is a frown
When you're upside down
And some people get my mood wrong

The Great Escape

A tortoise taken to his vet
Was nervous, as they are
And so he made a break for it
To get back to his car

Within ten minutes he was out
And stood by some dog's paw
He'd only made it from the box
Still had to scale the floor

Another half an hour meant
He'd made it past the chairs
Though only one thought crossed his mind
At least there were no stairs

Disaster struck when he was free
As someone saw him leave
At least he got a clap and cheer
For what he did achieve

Knitting Kneedles

I get a jumper from my Gran
She knits a new one every year
And though it seems a boring gift
The thanks I give her are sincere

I'm told she spends a whole three days
Ensuring it's a perfect fit
She won't go out or get the phone
The only thing she'll do is knit

The colours always seem to clash
And every year the style's the same
Inside will always have a place
To sew a tag that shows my name

But as she spends so long on it
I treasure what she's done for me
And when she's had her time on earth
They'll all be precious memories

On Ya Bike

The bike helps me get around town
If I go out far
I'll jump in the car
But traffic just makes me feel down

So if I'm in need of a tart
Or biscuits and cheese
I'll pass jams with ease
And pedalling's good for the heart

Sombre Story

As I was walking through the woods
Beside a mellow stream
A young man looked like he was in
The middle of a dream

I looked and saw he was awake
But seemed a little sad
And so I stopped and asked about
The kind of day he'd had

He said he wasn't happy as
His mum had news for him
As such a massive fan of frogs
He found it all quite grim

I had to ask what he had heard
That made him feel so down
Reluctantly he told his tale
Through one almighty frown

I now know that this poor guy's mum
Had meant it as a joke
When she told him that every frog
Eventually will croak

Project

There's rust living on every part
The doors are both loose
From brutal abuse
The battery shows from it's heart

The glass in each window is smashed
The tyres are flat
It hasn't one mat
The roof looks like it has been trashed

The paintwork is far from pristine
But money and time
Will make it look fine
It's worth it for this old machine

Gotta Laugh

I'm best known for my awful jokes
That often lack in taste
To go a day without a sound
For me's a total waste

I love to tell a groany gag
That makes you tut and sigh
I only hope that when I'm gone
My jokes will never die

Organised

I've sorted my whole wedding day
The bridesmaids and meal
All make this seem real
I won't even mind when I pay

I've found a great place with a room
I'll party all night
While still wearing white
The last thing I need is the groom

Two For The Zoo

I had to take my sister out
Although she's only four years old
We went out to our local zoo
Despite it being much too cold

We wrapped up warm with scarves and hats
As it's much cheaper than in June
I had enough to get us in
And some to buy her a balloon

I always keep my eye on her
But she slipped out of my tight grip
She got onto the penguin's slide
And made one of the poor birds trip

She ran her hand along the fence
That runs along the Lion's cage
This made him jump and roar out loud
She sent that cat into a rage

The Monkeys, Tigers and the Birds
All felt the wrath of this young girl
If she had been beneath the sea
She'd make the Oyster lose his pearl

We got her back eventually
She got stuck by the Kangaroo
Now I'm in trouble, but I'm sure
That she belongs inside the zoo

Window Wide Web

A fly caught in a spider's trap
Concerned for it's plight
Since ending it's flight
While hoping close by is a map

The fly tries to shake and escape
But there's no way out
And it dare not shout
This web is much worse than fly tape

The fly is in really deep now
The spider appears
Confirming it's fears
It knows it must get out somehow

The fly sees it's his lucky day
The spider has pies
Which he shares with flies
Before helping them go on their way

Coyote Sticky

Last night a lonely stick insect
Went partying 'til dawn
He woke this morning feeling ill
On someone's well kept lawn

He thought he'd hit the jackpot, but
His friends all called him thick
The lovely girl who lay by him
Was just a normal stick

On His Way In

The boss is late
He says the traffic was so tough
But we don't care
That poor excuse is not enough

If it were us
We'd make sure that we stayed in late
Though as it stands
The boss would have to work 'til eight

Yet once again
He gets away with this scot-free
And when he's in
He's sure to take it out on me

For this short time
While he's wrapped up in scarf and fleece
We'll have some fun
Indulging in this sacred peace

Constant

Our new baby smiles all the time
At least that's how it seems
When sleeping it's quite obvious
She's viewing happy dreams

It makes my wife want even more
Until our house is full
Though I don't think that our machine
Could cope with all the wool

The good thing is she'll change her mind
When faced with 'nappy crime'
Or when our baby screams for food
Which seems like all the time

Precedent

A fox saw his lawyer one pleasant Thursday
Concerned that soon hunting would chase him away
He wanted the hunters to give him some peace
And get compensation so this sport would cease

The lawyer sat down with a small glass of port
And said "This will never stand up in a court!"
The fox looked downtrodden, 'til his lawyer said
"Just tell them they hunt you while you're still in bed"

A case was arranged for ol' foxy to state
"We haven't a chance to escape this cold fate"
The hunters looked puzzled, and then they replied
"We can't even get to your bed" – foxy sighed

"Your dogs can" he said with a frown on his face
The judge was so shocked at this awful disgrace
He couldn't ban hunting, that wasn't his call
But what he awarded made our fox stand tall

"Two million pounds and you leave him alone"
The money would get him a massive new home
He walked out the courtroom a happier guy
Though hunting was legal which made his wife cry

But after a short time it wasn't to be
As foxy and family lived on happily
The old sport of hunting was then put on pause
As protesters fought for our old friend's lost cause

Miserable Achievement

I've won another holiday
My second in ten years
I got the letter yesterday
And read it through my tears

I really should be happier
As it won't cost a dime
But since it's only down the road
It seems a waste of time

BLiNd DrUNk

Staggering up to our front gate
Trying to find the right door key
Dodging the stones that line our path
Wishing I'd stuck to cups of tea

Knowing my girlfriend's waiting up
Probably with a rolling pin
Struggling to unlock the door
Willing the lock to let me in

Giving up as I'm too far gone
Watching my neighbour stagger, too
Finding out it's my drunk girlfriend
Merry and limping with one shoe

Trypanophobia

I've got a needle phobia
Which surely can't be rare
It only really shows itself
With hypodermics bare

There's quite a subtle irony
Attached to my great fear
By working in a Pharmacy
You'd think that it would clear

In Line

This queue isn't moving at all
There's only one till
That's open, but still
This guy should move faster than c-r-a-w-l

I wish they'd employ some more staff
As sales would go
To PROFIT from SLOW
And it would cut waiting by half

I'll stay for a few minutes more
Oh look, there's some socks
I'll pick up a box
I didn't see them there before…

Two's Company

My twin and I like playing tricks
On people who come round
The look they have upon their face
Is worth a thousand pounds

Although it may seem rather cruel
It makes us feel like Gods
We sometimes spend entire days
Pretending to be quads

My Way Of Life

I sit here in my rented flat
No company except my rat
We don't go out, just watch the box
With baskets full of dirty socks

There's pizza on the kitchen side
It's something I won't try to hide
Although this place may look a mess
I treat it as my own fortress

Though paint is peeling I don't care
And if it falls I'll leave it there
This may seem very strange to you
But visitors are very few

However, once a month I'll clean
And where I live will look pristine
I'll even cook a healthy tea
As mum comes round to visit me

Unexpected Break

There's no more work for me this week
In fact I can't go back
Through no fault of my own at all
My boss gave me the sack

I'd never work as long or fast
Or accurate as Bob
That new computer manages
Machines that have my job

Quiiiiiick!

Stand
Run
Ring my Dad
Talk
"Bye!"
Run like mad
Snack
Boil
Use the loo
Tea
Milk
Sugars, two
Walk
Dodge
Mind the chairs
Stop
Look
Down the stairs
Through
Up
Slice of cake
Ten
Minute
Coffee break

Down Through The Ages

Another story comes my way
From my grandparents' youth
They did so much when growing up
And only speak the truth

They tell me things that happened when
Their friends and them went out
And hope that we can learn from them
To see what life's about

I know they want what's best for me
But they bore me to tears
I only hope I'm interesting
When I can match their years

Stationary Swimmers (Haiku)

Swimming in the sand
None of us have realised
The tide has gone out

Choccy Biccy

The chocolate biscuits happy life
Begins inside a field
It's here that farmers pray each night
To gain a worthwhile yield

From there a tractor picks them up
And takes them to a place
It's best known as a factory
With lots of belts and space

Inside the walls of this new home
The biscuits get their shape
They get their taste and texture, too
And some will get a cape

They're taken to a shop by truck
A rough and dark ol' ride
But when they reach that sacred place
They're put on shelves inside

Some people buy them at the till
To take them to their house
They're boxed with pasties, burnt with tea
And end as someone's crouse

Redundancy Of The Reaper

Today's the Grim Reaper's last day
Although he won't mope
He'll now have to cope
With cash from his severance pay

Meaningful Existence

You want to make your life worthwhile
By doing something grand
To justify the time you spent
Upon this selfish land

An act that makes all others blush
Is what you said to me
Your life to now is not enough
But I must disagree

One action that you thought about
Was saving someone's life
But you saved mine the very day
I first called you my wife

The Best I Can Do

I've made something for granddad
His birthday is today
I couldn't get a new car
My mum told me "No way!"

I'm on my way to his house
With mum and dad in tow
I've wrapped his present nicely
With ribbon and a bow

I hope that he enjoys it
He likes the things I make
But mum has gone one better
She's made and iced a cake

I'm getting really nervous
And shaking to my toes
We're right outside his house now
And going in – here goes…

Away From The Crowds

I walk along the beach sometimes
When rain is pouring down
The wet stuff seems to tempt people
To wander through the town

I hate to be in dripping crowds
It never helps my health
But nothing's better than this sight
The whole beach to myself

Changing Weather

A cloudy, black sky welcomes me
Into this morning
A solemn warning
As I lock the door with the key

The clouds move like snails on sleet
There's no wind or breeze
Just air that would freeze
I think of my room, warm and sweet

Then, as the thought enters my mind
The clouds move away
Blue skies replace grey
And light rises up from behind

The sun lights and warms my whole path
My face grows a smile
That stretches a mile
My day brightens up as I laugh

In Too Deep

My training ended late last week
I work on submarines
It's been my dream to land this job
Since I was in my teens

There's only one small flaw with me
By small I mean immense
Most people have a fear of heights
But depths make me go tense

Searching For You

I wake to find that you're not there
It's just me in this bed we share
And though through weary eyes I peep
There's nobody where you would sleep

I call to find out where you are
While hoping that you're not too far
It troubles me to see you gone
An empty space where once you shone

I then resign as I well know
There's not a chance your face will show
I feel one final thought occur
You are not there, and never were

...Has Feelings Too

I find that people look at me
Like I'm some kind of freak
Which makes me want to run and hide
Though they see me as meek

I hate the way they point and stare
Before they nudge their mate
And then they call their family in
It gets me so irate

I'd love to go about my life
Without a single look
So I could sit out in the sun
And not behind a book

My friends have all abandoned me
As they can't take the heat
I've only got one friend these days
But he's a proper treat

Though this is now my destiny
I wish it wasn't true
As I know you'd feel awkward if
We Mermaids gawped at you

Verse Vica

There's good in evil and evil in good

A beautiful flower fights with all other plants
For food, water and light

The Devil welcomes thousands into his home
And he keeps the fire on all year

Certain Silence

A peace surrounds me in my room
The gentle type, untouched by gloom
A peace that shows how nothing moves
So soft and smooth it heals and soothes

A peace that's needed every day
To chase all crazy moods away
A peace that many never see
That makes a person feel so free

A peace to make all boredom die
As people sit and smile and sigh
A peace that causes some to weep
And sends me gently off to sleep

Chore Wars

I've done all that I need to do
And cleaned from top to toe
This morning was a crazy one
It's really been all go

I've sorted out the bathroom mess
And cleared the bedrooms too
The upstairs looked immaculate
But still I wasn't through

The kitchen was an awful state
Much worse than any room
A cup sat dormant on the side
Became an insect tomb

But now it's done my feet are up
So I can have some fun
I'll wait here 'til my family's back
And all my work's undone

'Lectric

Electricity running through
Unseen by us all
Kept safe in the wall
At hand when we've got things to do

It doesn't know how it will help
By lighting a lamp
Or running a camp
And heating the pan for your kelp

But though it may be a great friend
Just one broken cap
Combined with a zap
May lead to an untimely end

Not So Needy

When people notice Jake the dog
With three legs and no tail
They always spend some time with him
And stroke him without fail

The rest of us all envy him
Although this may seem crude
He lives behind a restaurant
And eats the finest food

Parent's Party

Snow outside to coat the path
People inside smile and laugh
Ready to exchange their gifts
As the room's excitement lifts

Children are all safe in bed
Can't forget what has been said
Santa Claus will come tonight
Once they sleep and there's no light

Adults gather with their friends
'Fore this festive season ends
With their work behind them all
They relax and have a ball

As the party nears it's close
Cameras capture every pose
Though they can't wait 'til next year
It's the children's turn to cheer

Fate

We try so hard when we leave home
To not be like our folks
We promise not to dance like fools
Or tell those stupid jokes

To save embarrassing our kids
Is one thing that we try
And so we hope they'll all approve
Of music that we buy

It's easy to convince ourselves
That we'll be good and kind
And when we give them barriers
They secretly won't mind

We look at how we got told off
For things that seemed so small
Like ripping our new trousers up
While climbing next door's wall

And so we swear to let them go
To run, explore and fight
Until they come back caked in mud
And prove our parents right

Hair Care

One solitary brunette hair
It lies on it's side
Not trying to hide
Or even pretend it's not there

It may not be real, just a fake
I care not a bit
As I watch it sit
Confined to the top of my cake

The Tale Of Loe Pool

The calmest lake you'll ever see
Where water's always still
Nobody round, which makes it seem
The perfect place to chill

A picturesque and gorgeous view
However it is seen
From beach or path, from up above
Or in the nearby green

Where ducks and swans will spend their time
When hiding from us all
Relaxing in secluded spots
Behind the reeds, so tall

But deep beneath the water's face
Where waves will not occur
There lies a demon hidden well
That makes the bottom stir

For anyone who wants a swim
Within this lake, untrue
Or even those who take their boat
Here's some advice for you

Each person whether seen or not
Who braves this evil deep
Has never lived to tell the tale
All they now know is sleep

Grim Reality

Their ugly eyes sit on their head
They leave a slime trail where they tread
The warts protrude from their wet back
And charm is something they all lack

They sit and look for flies to chew
With their long tongue they catch a few
They never clean their teeth or wash
Behaviour that makes us think 'Gosh!'

Yet they can always find a mate
Another toad who thinks they're great
Which shows that though we think they're odd
They hardly see us as their God

Fantasy...Spotted

Three unicorns were seen one day
Together by a trough
The spotter took a photograph
And quickly he sped off

The journalists all laughed aloud
When seeing his mistake
Of horses wearing party hats
While eating birthday cake

Creative Licence

Each word is like a masterstroke
And every line like fine detail
His notebook is his empty board
And this is how he tells his tale

'A picture's worth a thousand words'
He's heard this myth a hundred times
But when he paints his poetry
His fans are awed by his fresh rhymes

He won't be famous when he's gone
At best he might be quite well known
But still he writes to please himself
Content to know his work's his own

Teething Problems

When babies get their first few teeth
It drives the poor guys mad
They chew on everything in sight
Including Mum and Dad

They'll chew their toys and then the dog
Their plates and toy drum kit
They'll even chew on visitors
Who popped in for a bit

No ornament in sight is safe
From this electric saw
With tooth marks tainting everything
They'll still look round for more

Their folks will chase them round the house
Until they're out of breath
To give their child a teething ring
Which they'll suck half to death

Bad Timing

The inspiration seeps from me
Oh, why is it when
I don't have a pen
That I let my mind run so free?

The characters develop fast
I won't see it long
This image, so strong
I just hope, for once, it will last

A piece of white chalk and a floor
They'll do - but my mind
Has left them behind
Now, what did they look like before?

One Wind

The breeze turns to a gale force wind
And blows the branches round
When suddenly one breaks clean off
And falls straight to the ground

The branch that falls, a heavy one
As often these things are
Will find it's final resting place
Atop my brand new car

From You To Me

You've given me a ring before
With cufflinks for my brand new suit
And for our anniversary
A plant pot shaped just like a boot

I've had new films to watch with you
And music that you know I like
When I was offered my new job
You went and bought a brand new bike

You always know just what to get
To put a smile upon my face
And though my taste will change in time
Your gifts keep up despite the pace

Of all the things you've given me
There's one thing that I hold most dear
And that's the love you have for me
That's there at any time of year

Make That A Diet

I'm eating lettuce for this week
And nothing else at all
I need to lose a lot of weight
Before the summer ball

It may be hard but I'll succeed
A week is not that bad
It's like combining all the diets
That I have ever had

It's been a day and I feel weak
I've got to go to bed
Perhaps I'll have a decent meal
And start next week instead

Faithful Souls

Wherever we go they'll be there
Our every moment they will share
Supporting us through thick and thin
They'll be our platform when we win

Though friends may never be around
They'll keep our feet firm on the ground
And they are never jealous when
We choose another over them

Their comfort is a welcome charm
They're known to keep us safe from harm
They'll change to suit the way we feel
If we hurt them it's no big deal

They are the pals that we forget
Who suffer most when it is wet
No matter which pair you may choose
Just give a thought for your poor shoes

Surprise Party

The cheers and laughs are obvious
As I approach the door
They haven't all gone silent yet
So 'hush' is called once more

A meal is what they've brought me for
Though I know that's not true
I told them not to cause a fuss
And this is what they do

I open up to go on through
And they all shout "SURPRISE!"
Although I knew about this one
I still must dry my eyes

One Of Those Days

The car won't start
It's got no fuel
I'll never get
My kids to school

We'll have to walk
It's just a mile
But they're so down
I fake a smile

Some parents pass
And look at us
Tomorrow we
Will catch the bus

They didn't help
Us with a lift
That attitude
Is such a gift

We're nearly there
Inside the gate
We're running in
As we're so late

Huge Part

I've got a fine role in a film
As I'm the lead girl's Dad
This has to be the greatest part
That I have ever had

I've played a homeless man before
And one twin in a play
I've also been a hairdresser
For two weeks back in May

I'm hoping this will give me cred
Within the acting crowd
Which means I'll have to say my line
With meaning and quite loud

The Easy Life

I think babysitting's a cinch
When they're in their bed
Both warm and well fed
Without enough power to flinch

I've taken a job for tonight
It starts around eight
Miss Brown has a date
I'm sitting for her little mite

I've got DVD's and some food
It's just like at home
Though I'm on my own
So I'm in a happier mood

I get there and hear "THAT'S ENOUGH!"
Miss Brown then storms out
And there's a loud shout
My night's gone from easy to tough

Fad

I've fast become the latest craze
The toy that all kids need
By beating others to this post
My sales shot up with speed

I'm played with after each day's through
When they've come home from school
As I am introduced to friends
I hear the same word – "Cool!"

But soon my batteries will fail
And I'll be put down then
To be forgotten, lost, unloved
And never touched again

Act Of War

The sound of war had filled the stage
Events to alter this fine age
The actors sat within their pits
Attempting to avoid the hits

The other players sat across
To limit any kind of loss
Although the props were fairly poor
They matched their enemies for sure

No dress rehearsal was put on
No script was there to show who won
The best performance on the night
Decided who had won the fight

But at the end there were no smiles
No ceremony seen for miles
Nobody looked towards their crowd
As no-one clapped, and no-one bowed

The ones that made it back safely
All hoped to see their family
While now they've finished with the set
Here's one show they will not forget

Dress To Impress

Ladies wearing the same outfit
Arriving in one place
Will always look embarrassed, with
A stony, flushed red face

They'll sneer across the room all night
And won't have any fun
Because they bought their dress with hope
They'd be the only one

Nobody in this meeting place
Will know the anger felt
As both the ladies wish they'd worn
Long trousers with a belt

But if two men both look the same
There'll be no big dispute
The only thing you'll hear from them
Will be "Hey mate – nice suit"

De-stress

I take an hour out each day
Imagining I'm on a boat
And everything just disappears
So all I have to do is float

I have no phone beside my hand
So no-one can get hold of me
And nobody knocks at my door
As I am too far out to sea

It's something I look forward to
And even though it has to end
As all my stress floods back, I know
Tomorrow I'll be there again

Fluffy Terror

A black cloud floats across the sky
With only one intent
To ruin anything it finds
As this one is no gent

It notices a jumble sale
With children having fun
They're playing on the outdoor games
And bathing in the sun

The barbeque just seals the deal
It's really cooking well
Attracting people all the time
By sending out it's smell

The adults are oblivious
To this impending threat
They haven't got provisions out
To stop stalls getting wet

And so the cloud surprises them
By slowly passing by
Releasing everything it holds
And laughing as kids cry

As always with events like this
A hero must unfold
He takes the shape of someone's Dad
Who risks a nasty cold

As quickly as the cloud came past
This hero's back outside
By now the villain's well in place
And cannot run or hide

The hoover starts, a scene ensues
And soon the cloud's no more
The others watching clap and cheer
As they come through the door

Now good has triumphed once again
Although they were quite scared
And lessons have been learnt from this
Next time they'll be prepared

Final Stage

When you can feel that death is close
But still you know you're hanging on
When all around you seems so calm
Although you're sure you've not yet gone

When time begins to fade away
And life itself has said goodbye
When feelings darken in your mind
With just one final question - Why?

When family make your pain their own
By helping out with every need
When fantasies you've always held
Become no more than rotten greed

You'll know then what your place was here
The reason you were put on earth
And how you helped mankind evolve
However small, to now from birth

Last One

The final chocolate in the box
That dreaded whisky cream
To be picked out before the rest
Is nothing but a dream

It wouldn't even mind so much
If all the rest were great
But people eat the toffees first
Which makes this choc irate

Near here

A lake that sits out of the way
A tranquil place throughout the day
Where people hire boats to row
And ducks and swans are there on show

With swings, a slide and seesaw too
There's plenty there for all to do
The scenery's a special sight
And looks so good in any light

The walk around this calming lake
Is something one and all should take
This place has really made it's mark
It's name is Coronation Park

Doctor's Orders

I have to go to AA meets
As drink's got hold of me
But surely since it's Rum And Coke
I need the RAC

So Close, So Far

She killed me the day that she went
To stay with her Mum
Although she looked glum
She took all her things plus my tent

I'm roaming around feeling lost
Told work I was sick
It wouldn't be quick
And now I'm left counting the cost

I have so much round me to do
She's gone and I'm glad
But I still feel mad
I wish that she took the kids, too

Since We Last Met

If you know me you can't have missed
That I've put on some weight
You may have even mentioned that
I look an awful state

Although you see an elephant
When I walk through the door
I'll never hide away in shame
That's not what my life's for

Distant Love

You live just out of my home town
I watch you from so far away
No matter who I'm with or where
I think about you every day

You've always been so out of reach
But you're the only one for me
I cannot bear this time apart
Though we have not touched physically

I can at last declare my love
To you, who keeps my heart afloat
As on this day I have enough
To purchase you, my brand new boat

If Only…

My final day upon this earth
Began with buttered toast
I left my house the normal time
And missed the morning post

If I'd have read my letters first
I'd know I won the pools
Instead I took a fatal route
To bypass local schools

My car slipped on a coastal road
Through no fault of my own
I went straight through a barrier
From which my car was thrown

I may have died a wealthy man
Though no-one knew to care
The letter was destroyed intact
But who said life was fair?

Gradient

I walk the hill
Knowing great things wait at the top
Though my feet start to ache I walk through the pain

Further I go
My legs feel like they may fall off
It doesn't help that I'm walking in the rain

I'm past halfway
Starting to forget my purpose
And why I'm climbing this hill in the first place

Someone passes
They know that it's at the top, too
However I must carry on, it's not a race

Close to the top
The other guy must have reached it
Hopefully he hasn't noticed that it's there

Made it at last!
It must have been taken away
It was right here, but where it sat is now bare

Proper Planning

There's oil between the min and max
Or so the dipstick shows
The radiator's topped right up
And not one warning glows

I've filled the windscreen fluid up
The wipers both work well
We're now all ready to set off
As far as I can tell

With all the checks that I have done
It really pains me that
I'm stopped beside the motorway
Because my tyre's flat

Waiting Up

Eighteen hours she's been away
It's now become another day
But she has not called me all night
To let me know that she's alright

She could be lost or stuck or worse
Someone could chase her for her purse
But still I sit and worry here
For one quick call to say she's near

I'm sure that I'll stop crying soon
And look for her beneath this moon
Though I know once I leave our place
I'll miss her scared and tired face

Nobody wants to know just yet
As one full day is what they've set
So it's right here that I'll remain
The tension driving me insane

Mi Padre

Mi Padre es mi amigo
Mi Padre es especial
Mi Padre es tan cómico
Mi Padre no es Español

My Parent's Trip

We're going for a tough, long hike
Along the hills and mountain tops
And we can't even use a bike
Although we've planned a few short stops

It's not a route I've done before
Or anywhere I know too well
Which clothes I'll wear, I'm not quite sure
And when we'll get back - who can tell?

It's time to set off on our trip
Across the rough tracks and terrain
Avoiding each large hole and dip
I really hope it doesn't rain

Now we are halfway through the rough
And Dad is tearing out his hair
I think my Mum's had quite enough
She's turned me round in my pushchair

Longest Part Of The Day

Ten minutes left 'til I go home
I watch the clock count down
I've got so much to do tonight
At home and in the town

I wish the boss would let me go
There's no more work to do
It's just me and that time device
From now until work's through

There is no point in doing more
I'll sit and watch that face
Besides, there's just nine minutes left
Then I can leave this place

Wooded Walk

We've set off to the woods for a walk
By starting at nine
We caught the sunshine
And there's time to just dawdle and talk

As the group carry on through the trees
Doubt crosses my mind
So I drag behind
With the wind picking up from a breeze

Now I'm certain we've wandered off course
This trail seems new
Our troop's seen it, too
But our leader's trekked on through the gorse

After telling us not to go back
He's marched on ahead
And taken the bread
If he doesn't return we'll all crack

A quick glance to the right brings a smile
We're right by the car
It doesn't look far
The relief makes the walk seem worthwhile

A.M. Commute

The morning traffic's hideous
We never seem to move
What's worse is when the other cars
Have something they must prove

By shouting at their driving peers
They always fail to see
Exactly how ridiculous
It looks to you and me

But still we put up with the taunts
And stupid things they say
Because we'll get a mini break
From them on Saturday

Sunset

Crimson Tides
Touched with glowing
A cooling breeze
Hardly showing

Hilltops dull
Where once they shone
The whole sea calm
The tide near gone

Dark sunlight
Which paints the sky
Pink and orange
'Til night comes by

Watching all
From on the sand
With you nearby
To hold my hand

Stunning scenes
We won't forget
As time stands still
For our sunset

Verse Readings

A poem always comes alive
When it's read out aloud
No matter what the venue size
Or volume of the crowd

A voice will strike the deepest chord
Within the hardest soul
And break the hearts of stony types
To leave a pleasant hole

All this is best remembered when
A poem finds your course
So find a friend to read it out
And you will feel this force

Familiar Strangers

The view from my window's an interesting one
I see people come and can see when they've gone
I watch as they walk in the gardens outside
And notice the children as they try to hide

I see different faces throughout my long day
And often I'll catch something someone might say
It's never unpleasant, the view from my flat
As I watch the dogs who, in turn, watch my cat

The people from town often give me a wave
I don't mind if they see me when I'm mid-shave
I'll happily watch them as they all walk past
Although some are rushing, and walk by so fast

I never go outside but I can still feel
Affection from passers that I know is real
And though I get visits from people I know
My life's all about what these good people show

When night skies draw in I'm quite safe in my bed
As I still have people alert when they tread
They're happy to check that my house is secure
And never walk off if they're feeling unsure

When Christmas arrives I will leave out some cake
The children all share it before I'm awake
And though in my heart I know life always ends
I'm making the most of my ten-second friends

Life For Others

She lived there for about six years
The orphanage in town
And anyone who looked at her
Would only ever frown

No adults helped her to grow up
She had to teach herself
This meant she really suffered with
Her learning and her health

Her hair was dry and knotted up
Her teeth were dull and weak
Her temperament remained so mild
They often called her meek

One day her luck completely changed
Somebody looked her way
They fell in love with who she was
And took her on that day

Now she remains so calm and warm
As peaceful as a dove
But she looks healthy and she smiles
Because of someone's love

My Lazy Day

The tide that day had come in late
The sea itself had kept so still
The sun was nowhere to be seen
As it stayed put behind the hill

Nobody walked around outside
No wind was present anywhere
The animals had all stayed in
It seems they were content in there

As everyone was out of sight
I stayed exactly where I lay
And rested in that gentle calm
Which still remains my greatest day

Employment Emporium

I couldn't do the job you do
And take abuse for helping out
When you just want to make them well
They pull away or punch and shout

I couldn't spend my time at work
Chasing hoaxes or even worse
Telling them you're not a taxi
Then watching them explode and curse

I'd never want to see the sight
Of children trapped inside a car
Or see a 'Baby On Board' sign
And wonder whereabouts they are

So praise goes out to you, my friend
Who's there to take the good and poor
As well as using normal sharps
While never falling to the floor

Movement Of The Cat

The cat will prowl about the house
His eyes wide and keen
A face stern and mean
To save his abode from the mouse

The silk-like, slow moves he will make
Are so well defined
To match the cat's mind
Which shows with each step he will take

When enemies enter his rooms
The cat will stay calm
And pounce with great charm
His prey rushing off as he grooms

Playing The Markets

My stocks have risen ultra high
So I have bought a plane
Now I can rise as high as them
Despite the wind and rain

I'm soaring like the grandest bird
Above the people's heads
Rejoicing in my quick gained wealth
While they sleep in their beds

Although my broker told me stock
Could rise as well as fall
I smile for him, stuck in his job
While I'm above them all

He said that stock was like a plane
One day it may lose 'flight'
And as the floor gets closer quick
I see now he was right

Transport Public

Whilst riding the bus
There's often a fuss
Over where everybody will sit

They shuffle and fight
All day and all night
And don't care for each other one bit

Some people will stay
On their seat all day
Without helping a person in need

If you're old or sick
You'd better be quick
Or you'll stand for the sake of their greed

I'll help if I can
But I'm just one man
And they're often aggressive with me

But they only shout
As I'll kick them out
Plus, as driver, my seat's always free

What Girls?

They float through in a brand new dress
As though they are a known actress
A champagne glass held high in hand
Behind the latest punk rock band

They smile and wave as people stare
To get a glimpse of them stood there
Their picture's taken as they go
Into the premiere or show

They always show their made-up eyes
And know how to accessorize
With bags and jewellery hanging down
To compliment their far out gown

But once they get back to their car
It's obvious they've gone too far
They trip up on their own two feet
For journalists it's such a treat

Pages Of My Journal

Day One – I have decided I
Will write down all my thoughts
The things I've seen and said and done
And any quick retorts

I'll write the things I won't forget
Events that brought me woe
The places I have visited
With funny things I know

Recording all my wisdom, though
Requires time and craft
To make sure I remember when
I cried or smiled or laughed

But now the introduction's done
It's time to get some rest
To make sure I am rested so
My journal is it's best

Day Fifty Eight – I'm sorry, friend
I've left your pages bare
However I'll be married soon
And won't have time to spare

Writer's Block (Haiku)

I class myself as
The most useful writer's block
I'm a paperweight

Special Place

The river runs beside the path
I hear the birds sat in the trees
The squirrels start to stir and wake
I feel the final chilly breeze

The meadow looks so lush and green
As sheep and cattle graze close by
The path is much more busy now
Due mainly to the cloudless sky

The hedge is home to early plants
That all try reaching for the sun
This is my favourite time of year
As Spring itself has just begun

I walk where only people go
The road is nowhere to be seen
A place where time does not exist
So calm and gentle, so serene

Post-Summer

It's getting darker sooner now
Which leaves me feeling low
The days are far too short for me
And nights fade much too slow

There isn't much that I can do
With light from garage lamps
My car will spend these winter months
With two wheels up on ramps

I'll have to find a different type
Of hobby for a while
And think of summer's sweet return
To help maintain my smile

Place To Hide

In our front room there is a box
With flowers inside
A great place to hide
And all that it's missing are locks

I've put the blooms down on the floor
Now I'm climbing in
By using the bin
I hope someone comes through the door

My dad's walked in - now I'll jump out
To give him a scare
What's that he's got there?
I'd better give up and just shout

He's taped up the box at the top
We're both in the car
This has gone too far
He didn't hear my cries to stop

I've suddenly come over ill
I need to get back
Or I'll start to crack
He's posted me out to Brazil

Symbolism

The pure white dove's a sign of peace
Across this Blue-Green land
It's offered when the battles cease
From cage to foe by hand

But does the dove know of this trend
And do they use it too?
Are humans offered at the end
When doves have a to-do?

The Birds And The Bees

The bird seems not to have a plan
Except, of course, avoiding Man
And finding something sweet to chew
Whilst in it's nest, well built and new

It's safe from danger as it flies
Between the trees and through the skies
And when it swoops it's always sure
There's something useful on the floor

Most days are spent on these few chores
Although occasionally I'm sure
A disco held within the trees
Means they can party with the bees

Home Sweet Home

I live on a houseboat
Floating out to sea
No-one else lives in here
There is only me

I don't want a mansion
Or a car or yacht
I am quite content with
All the things I've got

When I want to see friends
We meet at the coast
Sometimes they will look round
And bring me my post

I don't need a phone line
TV or a fax
Since I'm off the mainland
There's no council tax

The Cat's Away

We're causing a ruckus today
The boss has gone out
So can't hear us shout
Or see us lead others astray

It isn't too long that we're free
He's gone for a snack
Not long 'til he's back
Besides, we've got patients to see

Career Fears

I've had six jobs since I left school
Which was two years ago
I've been a life guard, printed books,
I've even shovelled snow

I've worked within an awful shop
I even held the key
But I found out before too long
The bosses hated me

I've never tried to be well paid
As that makes people change
I'm happy just to sit all day
With buds to re-arrange

I can remember ever since
I was a little boy
I've wanted to be good within
A job I can enjoy

I don't mind waiting if I must
'Til that job shows it's face
But I refuse to settle with
A dull and lifeless place

One Split Second

My eyes both widen in the lights
But I see nothing, just their glow
That yellow glare that steals my sight
The only noise is loud and low

I know that sound - of that I'm sure
Although it's not a common noise
It almost knocks me to the floor
Though it's my hearing it destroys

This all seems so familiar
Why do I recognise these signs?
I feel like I'm close to a car
And this footpath has painted lines

And then it dawns just where I am
I should be moving somewhere fast
But now I've caused a traffic jam
It's my fault that a truck just crashed

Never Forgotten

When I think of Robert Marshall
I think of Love and fun
His special gift of mayhem that
He gave to everyone

He'd always help me with my car
As it's all foreign to me
I watched in awe the time he put
An engine in my mini

Despite this he would never boast
Just smile 'til it was in
And tell me if he had the choice
My car would see the bin

But whether we would fight or laugh
About this or the other
By name he is my in-law, but
To me he is my brother

Broken Down

I bought a new car yesterday
The ad said 'Drive out straight away'
But as I got out of the town
I heard a bang and slowed right down

The whole exhaust had fallen off
The car gave out a hearty cough
Smoke bellowed out in one big cloud
Of this new car I was not proud

It took too long to move the beast
Once full of life, but now deceased
It would be written off for sure
As it's condition had no cure

Now I have got the cash for it
Not what I paid, but a fair bit
I haven't found a car I like
So I may quit and buy a bike

The Joy Of Six

All I think of is having Six
Wherever I may be
At work, at home or in the pub
The thought takes over me

My boss said I deserved a raise
And though I told him 'Yes'
I knew I'd give it up for Six
My world is such a mess

I have a healthy home life, too
With four kids and a wife
But sometimes all I want is Six
It's ruining my life

I know that when my time is through
I won't be quite so glum
My days will all be filled with Six
My paradise will come